Totally Into Fishing and Hunting

Turkey Hunting

Abby Badach Doyle

Gareth Stevens Publishing

Please visit our website, www.garethstevens.com. For a free color catalog of all our high-quality books, call toll free 1-800-542-2595 or fax 1-877-542-2596.

Cataloging-in-Publication Data
Names: Doyle, Abby Badach.
Title: Turkey hunting / Abby Badach Doyle.
Description: New York : Gareth Stevens Publishing, 2023. | Series: Totally into fishing and hunting | Includes glossary and index.
Identifiers: ISBN 9781538280157 (pbk.) | ISBN 9781538280171 (library bound) | ISBN 9781538280164 (6pack) | ISBN 9781538280188 (ebook)
Subjects: LCSH: Turkey hunting–Juvenile literature.
Classification: LCC SK325.T8 D69 2023 | DDC 799.2'4645–dc23

Portions of this work were originally authored by Jonathan Potter and published as *We're Going Turkey Hunting*. All new material in this edition is authored by Abby Badach Doyle.

Published in 2023 by
Gareth Stevens Publishing
29 East 21st Street
New York, NY 10010

Editor: Abby Badach Doyle
Designer: Michael Flynn

Photo credits: Cover, p. 1 Nahian Aronno/Shutterstock.com; series background (camo) Alexvectors/Shutterstock.com; p. 4 Kyle Wiles/Shutterstock.com; p. 5 thangs1/Shutterstock.com; pp. 7, 8 Michael Tatman/Shutterstock.com; p. 9 Jeffrey B. Banke/Shutterstock.com; p. 11 (eggs) Elias Glesmann/Shutterstock.com; p. 11 (hen) DesignTop/Shutterstock.com; p. 13 Gregory Crosby Jr/Shutterstock.com; p. 14 Natalila Maksymenko/Shutterstock.com; p. 15 Dmitry Markov152/Shutterstock.com; p. 17 (target) Evgenius1985/Shutterstock.com; p. 17 (turkey illustration) courtesy of National Wild Turkey Federation; p. 19 Dewayne Flowers/Shutterstock.com; p. 20 K Steve Cope/Shutterstock.com; p. 21 Bryan Eastham/Shutterstock.com; p. 23 (slate call) enterlinedesign/Shutterstock.com; p. 23 (box call) Stephanie Frey/Shutterstock.com; p. 24 David DeFillipo/Shutterstock.com; p. 25 Joseph M Wilson/Shutterstock.com; p. 27 Foxys Graphic/Shutterstock.com; p. 29 Beau Leyse/Shutterstock.com.

Printed in the United States of America

A NOTE TO READERS
Always talk with a parent or teacher before proceeding with any of the activities found in this book. Some activities require adult supervision.

A NOTE TO PARENTS AND TEACHERS
This book was written to be informative and entertaining. Some of the activities in this book require adult supervision. Please talk with your child or student before allowing them to proceed with any hunting activities. The author and publisher specifically disclaim any liability for injury or damages that may result from use of information in this book.

Some of the images in this book illustrate individuals who are models. The depictions do not imply actual situations or events.

CPSIA compliance information: Batch #CSGS23: For further information contact Gareth Stevens, New York, New York at 1-800-542-2595.

CONTENTS

WORDS IN THE GLOSSARY APPEAR IN BOLD TYPE THE FIRST TIME THEY ARE USED IN THE TEXT.

TURKEY TIME

Millions of people hunt wild turkeys in the United States every year. Turkeys are the second most popular U.S. animal to hunt, next to deer. Many hunters love the **challenge** of turkey hunting. Turkeys have great eyesight and can spot even very small movements.

KNOW THE FACTS!

Native Americans including the Mohawk, Huron, Onondaga, Shawnee, and Ojibwa Peoples hunted turkeys for their meat, but also used all parts of the animal. The Powhatan People used feathers for arrows and clothing. Bones were used for tools, beads, and whistles.

BONE WHISTLE

An adult male turkey is called a gobbler or tom.

The wild turkey is native to North America. Some Native Peoples, such as early Puebloans, viewed these birds as **sacred**. Today, turkey is the highlight of many Thanksgiving dinners. But you don't have to wait for November to enjoy this tasty bird!

IN THE WILD

In the wild, turkeys snack on grasses, acorns, berries, nuts, and seeds. They also eat small creatures and bugs, such as grasshoppers and cicadas. Cicadas are large, noisy bugs with wings.

Most of the turkey we eat comes from farms. Domestic, or farmed, turkeys eat feed made from corn or soybeans. They are larger with white feathers. Many hunters prefer the taste of wild turkey meat. It is leaner than domestic turkey meat. Plus, it is satisfying to eat something you worked hard to hunt.

KNOW THE FACTS!

Ask another hunter what turkeys like to eat in your area. Then, learn how to **identify** those plants and creatures. This can help you find a good hunting spot.

Wild turkeys are omnivores, which means they eat both plants and meat.

WHERE TO GO

Turkeys live in forests and grassy fields. During the day, they peck for food in the grass. At night, they fly up into trees to roost. Successful turkey hunters pick spots in the woods that offer clear views for shooting.

Many hunters hunt on state game lands, which are large natural areas owned by the government. Wild turkeys can also be hunted on private property if the owner allows it. Always ask before hunting on someone's land, and obey "no hunting" signs.

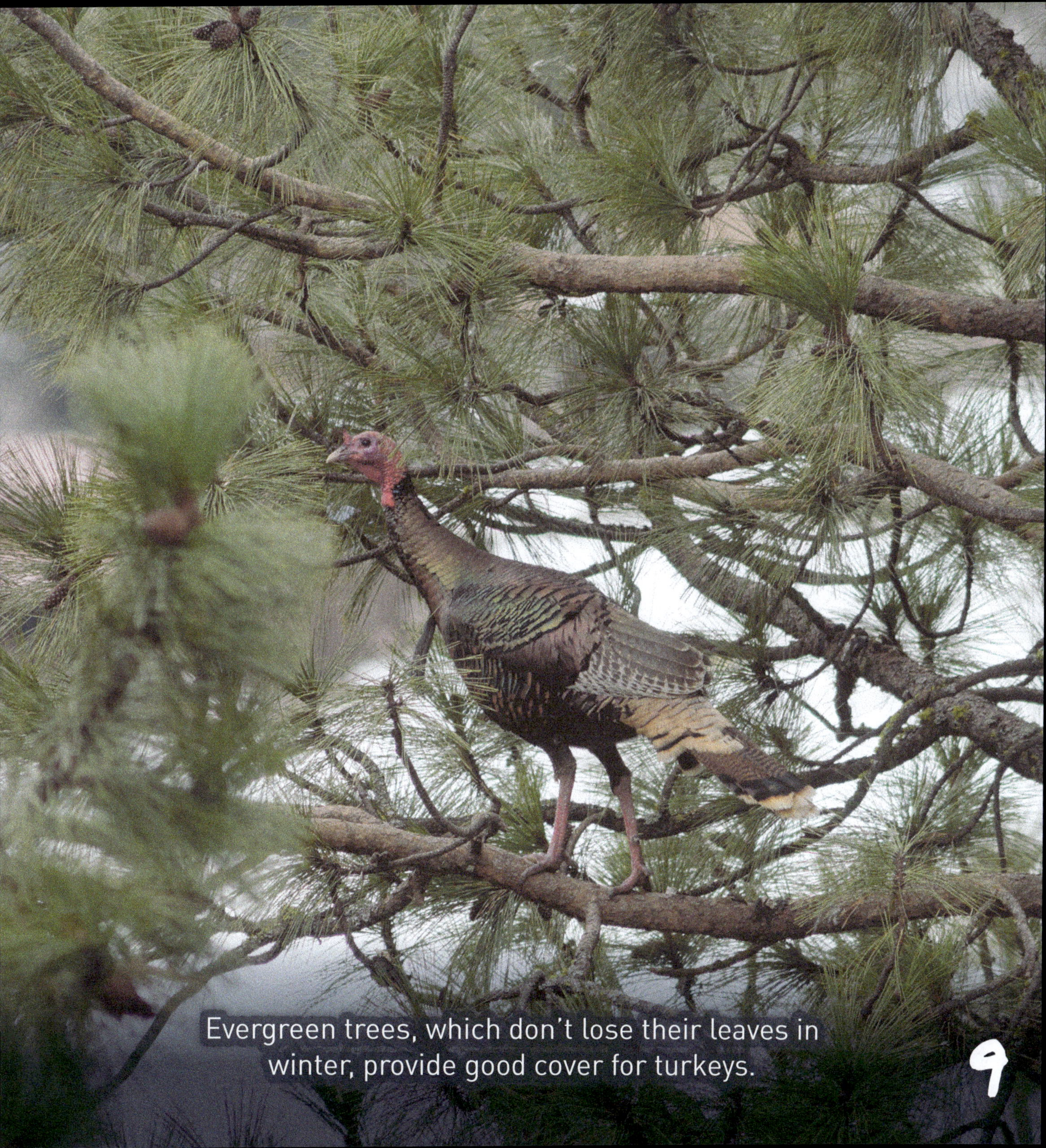

Evergreen trees, which don't lose their leaves in winter, provide good cover for turkeys.

FALL OR SPRING?

A hunting season is the time when you're allowed to hunt a certain animal. Like other game animals, turkeys are in season during the fall and sometimes winter. Most states also have spring gobbler seasons to hunt males. Spring is when turkeys are active to mate, or make babies.

Some hunters prefer one season over the other. Some hunters consider fall hunting to be more challenging. It can be harder to get gobblers to come to you in the autumn.

KNOW THE FACTS!

A young male turkey is called a jake. Not all states allow hunters to shoot jakes or hens. Some hunters just prefer not to, even if it is allowed.

A female turkey, called a hen, lays eggs once a year. Each nest can have 4 to 17 eggs.

BLEND IN

Turkeys can see color. This is different than other game animals, such as deer, which can't see certain colors. To stay hidden, turkey hunters often wear camouflage. This clothing has colors and shapes to help hunters blend in with the woods.

Some, but not all, states require hunters to wear bright orange. This helps other hunters to see them for safety. Some hunters wear orange when they move through the forest. When they stay still, they wear camouflage and mark a nearby tree with something orange.

KNOW THE FACTS!

When you go turkey hunting, avoid wearing red, white, or blue. Turkey heads have these colors. A hunter might mistake you for a gobbler in the forest.

A camouflage face mask and gloves help you stay hidden.

HUNTING WITH SHOTGUNS

Many hunters say a shotgun is the best firearm, or gun, to hunt turkeys. Shotguns shoot shells that are tightly packed with small pellets called shot. The shot explodes out of the gun and scatters in a small area.

KNOW THE FACTS!

Never point a gun at yourself or another person, even just to joke around. A hunting safety course will teach you how to use a firearm safely.

You'll need to clean your gun occasionally to keep it working well.

Shotguns have a shorter range than rifles, which are long guns held against the shoulder. To get a good shot, a hunter must get close to a turkey. A turkey is considered "in range" when it gets 40 yards (36.6 m) away.

TARGET PRACTICE

A target is where you direct your effort when you shoot. Sporting clubs often have shooting ranges where hunters can practice on a target shaped like a turkey. At a shooting range, you will learn how to hold your gun and position your feet.

Before you hunt, make sure you practice shooting from different positions. It's also important to pattern your shotgun. This is when you shoot a paper target. Then, you measure where the shot hits to make sure your gun fires where you aim.

KNOW THE FACTS!

When shooting with a firearm, aim at the head and neck area of the turkey. Shooting the bird here will kill it cleanly with the least amount of suffering.

A turkey's neck is small and moves a lot.
It is a challenging target!

HUNTING WITH BOWS

You can also hunt turkeys with a bow and arrow. This is also called archery. Modern **compound** bows are more advanced than the bows and arrows of the past. They have cables and **pulleys** that make it easier to pull back an arrow.

Broadhead arrowheads are the best for turkey hunting. They are shaped like triangles with sharp edges. Bowhunters must have excellent aim to hit their target. You'll need to practice using a bow before heading off on a hunt.

KNOW THE FACTS!

It takes a lot of movement to draw, or pull back, your arrow. This is hard to do without a turkey noticing. Some hunters hide in blinds, or small tents, when hunting.

When bowhunting, you have to get much closer to get a good shot.

GETTING STARTED

Whether you hunt with a bow or a shotgun, you'll need to take a safety course. You may also need a hunting **license**. A hunting safety course will teach you how to handle your gun or bow, **responsible** treatment of animals, and first aid.

If you can, explore the land you want to hunt on before turkey season begins. You can look for signs of turkeys, like tracks and droppings. It also helps to get familiar with the land so you don't get lost on hunting day.

Leaning on a large rock or tree **supports** your back and hides you from turkeys.

TURKEY CALLS

Calls are used to imitate, or copy, the sounds made by turkeys. Some hunters use calls to trick turkeys into coming closer. You can call using a tool or just your mouth and hands. Turkeys do more than gobble. They also yelp, purr, and cluck. Each sound means something different.

The best hunters know how to make the right call at the right time. Be careful, though. Calls can also fool hunters. If you think another hunter is nearby, you shouldn't make turkey calls.

KNOW THE FACTS!

Some hunters get very skilled at turkey calling. There are **competitions** where you can go up against other turkey callers. You can win money and prizes!

Turkey calls are small enough to take with you when you hunt.

DECOYS

Decoys look like real turkeys, but they're fake. Decoys catch the attention of real turkeys to draw them closer to you. Turkey decoys can look like hens, jakes, or toms. Hunters can use more than one decoy at a time.

It's best to put your decoys in an open field. That gives you space to take a clean shot. For safety, always cover a decoy when you carry it. You don't want another hunter shooting at a decoy while it's in your hands.

You can put actual turkey feathers on your decoy to make it look more real.

GOT ONE!

Once you shoot a turkey, the next step is to field dress it. Field dressing cools the animal's body by removing its **organs**. This keeps the meat from going bad. Bring a sharp knife, garbage bags, and plastic gloves for field dressing.

To prepare the meat to eat, you can take out the bird's feathers or remove all its skin. If you see any shot pellets, pick them out. Finally, fill out the tag from your hunting license. This form helps your state keep track of turkey populations.

KNOW THE FACTS!

Lead is a metal used in some types of shot. Lead can make people and animals sick when eaten. Choose shells made from other metals, such as iron, tin, copper, or steel.

CUTS OF TURKEY

You can cook your turkey whole or cut it into parts. Cutting up an animal to prepare it to eat is called butchering. Each cut of turkey meat has its own name.

HEALTHY POPULATIONS

In the early 1900s, wild turkeys nearly died out. People overhunted them and destroyed their **habitats**. Only about 30,000 birds remained. Groups such as the National Wild Turkey Federation (NWTF) have worked hard to bring the turkey back. A federation is a group that joins together smaller groups that care about the same thing.

More than 6 million turkeys are alive today. Money from hunting licenses and taxes helps pay for **conservation** programs. These aim to keep turkey populations healthy for years to come.

KNOW THE FACTS!

Good hunters respect wildlife and care about nature. Hunters such as President Theodore Roosevelt have helped create laws to keep animals and habitats safe.

The National Wild Turkey Federation has been around since 1973.

GLOSSARY

challenge: a test of abilities

competition: an event in which people try to win

compound: made up of two or more parts

conservation: the care of the natural world

habitat: the place or type of place where a plant or animal naturally or normally lives or grows

identify: to find out the name or features of something

license: a piece of paper that allows someone to do something

organ: a part inside an animal's body

pulley: a wheel or group of wheels that is combined with a rope or chain to lift and lower objects

responsible: able to be trusted to do what is right or to do the things that are expected or required

sacred: specially blessed

support: to hold up and help

FOR MORE INFORMATION

BOOKS

Carpenter, Tom. *Upland Bird Hunting.* Lake Elmo, MN: Focus Readers, 2017.

Roe, Monica. *Turkey Hunt Tradition.* North Mankato, MN: Capstone, 2022.

WEBSITES

Hunter-Ed

hunter-ed.com

View study guides and take state-approved hunting safety courses online.

Wild Turkey Sounds

nwtf.org/hunt/wild-turkey-basics/turkey-sounds

Listen to the different sounds wild turkeys make so you can practice your calls.

INDEX